How do they work?

Toy Cars

Wendy Sad...

Heinemann LIBRARY

young Explorer

www.heinemann.co.uk/library

Visit our website to find out more information about **Heinemann Library** books.

To order:

☎ Phone 44 (0) 1865 888066

▤ Send a fax to 44 (0) 1865 314091

▢ Visit the Heinemann Bookshop at www.heinemann.co.uk/library to browse our catalogue and order online.

First published in Great Britain by Heinemann Library, Halley Court, Jordan Hill, Oxford OX2 8EJ, part of Harcourt Education.
Heinemann is a registered trademark of Harcourt Education Ltd.

© Harcourt Education Ltd 2005
First published in paperback in 2006
The moral rights of the author and proprietor have been asserted.

Editorial: Andrew Farrow and Dan Nunn
Design: Ron Kamen and Dave Oakley/
 Arnos Design
Picture Research: Hannah Taylor
Production: Duncan Gilbert
Originated by Ambassador Litho Ltd
Printed and bound in China by
South China Printing Company.

The paper used to print this book comes from sustainable resources.

10 digit 0 431 04967 X (Hardback)
13 digit 978 0 431 04967 0 (Hardback)
09 08 07 06 05
10 9 8 7 6 5 4 3 2

10 digit 0 431 04974 2 (Paperback)
13 digit 978 0 431 04974 8 (Paperback)
10 09 08 07 06
10 9 8 7 6 5 4 3 2 1

British Library Cataloguing in Publication Data

Sadler, Wendy
  Toy cars. – (How do they work?)
  1. Automobiles – Models – Design and construction – Juvenile literature
  2. Motor vehicles – Models – Design and construction – Juvenile literature
  I. Title
  688.7'28

A full catalogue record for this book is available from the British Library.

Acknowledgements

The publishers would like to thank the following for permission to reproduce photographs:
Alamy Images pp. **15** (Superstock), **25** (Deborah Chadbourne); Getty Images (Taxi) p. **26**; Harcourt Education Ltd (Tudor Photography) pp. **4**, **5**, **6**, **7**, **8**, **9**, **10**, **11**, **12**, **13**, **14**, **16**, **17**, **18**, **19**, **20**, **21**, **22**, **23**, **24**, **28–29**; Zefa (R. Holz) p. **27**.

Cover photograph reproduced with permission of Harcourt Education Ltd (Tudor Photography).

Every effort has been made to contact copyright holders of any material reproduced in this book. Any omissions will be rectified in subsequent printings if notice is given to the publishers.

Contents

Some words are shown in bold, **like this**. You can find out what they mean by looking in the glossary.

 Find out more about toy cars at www.heinemannexplore.co.uk

Toy cars

Toy cars come in all shapes and sizes. Some are small enough to fit into your hand. Others are big enough to sit on.

Toy cars roll along the ground on their wheels. Most cars have four wheels, one at each corner. Some cars have more wheels.

Wheels

wheel

Wheels help a toy car to move. This toy truck has lost some of its wheels. Without these, it cannot roll along the ground.

wheel

Wheels keep the body of a car off the ground. The car can go over small bumps and holes without getting stuck.

7

Wheels are round

the wheels turn like this

Look at the shape of the wheels
on these cars. All of the wheels
are round. The wheels turn as the
cars roll across the floor.

This car has square wheels. The wheels would not turn round if you tried to move the car. The corners of the squares would get in the way. This means the car cannot roll.

Tyres

wheel

tyre

Tyres are things that fit around the outside of wheels. They help the wheels **grip** the ground. Tyres on toy cars are made of rubber or plastic.

wheel

rubber tyre squashes

Rubber changes shape, or squashes,
when you push it. Rubber tyres make
the ground seem less bumpy.

Axles

axle

wheels and axle turn at the same time

Wheels are joined to **axles**. A wheel would not go round if it was stuck to the car with glue. On this toy car, the axle turns inside the car. This means both the axle and the wheels go round at the same time.

axle is fixed to car and cannot turn

each wheel can turn by itself

On this toy car, the axle is fixed tightly to the car and cannot turn. The wheels turn, but the axle does not. This means each wheel can turn by itself.

13

Making cars move

the car is
pushed this way

the car
moves forwards

Some cars cannot go by themselves. To
make them move you have to push them
or pull them. You are using a **force** to
make the car move.

the cart is pulled
this way

the cart moves
forwards

This cart is being pulled to make it
move. If no one pulled or pushed
the cart, it would not go anywhere.

15

Going up and down

push

It takes a big **force** to make a car move up a slope. This means that a car going uphill needs a big push! If the girl lets go of the car, it will roll back down the slope.

the car moves
down the slope

gravity

A car can travel down a hill without being pushed. A force called **gravity** pulls the car down the slope towards the ground. You cannot see gravity, but it is always working.

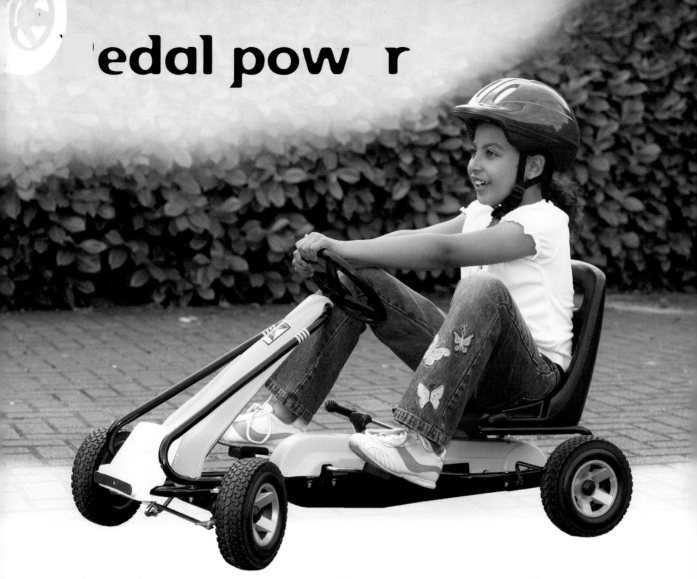

edal pow r

This toy car uses the movement of the girl's legs and feet to make it go. The pedals are joined to the wheels. When she moves her feet, the pedals make the wheels go round.

18

lever

pedal   wheel

The pedals are joined to a long stick called a **lever**. The lever makes it easier to make the wheels go round.

19

Changing direction

push

When the wheels of a car are going round, the car can move forwards or backwards. It is hard to push a car sideways. The wheels do not go round in that direction.

20

Some toy cars have front wheels that can turn. When you turn the **steering wheel**, the front wheels of the car also turn. This means the car will be able to go round corners!

turning the steering wheel turns the wheels

the car changes direction

Clockwork cars

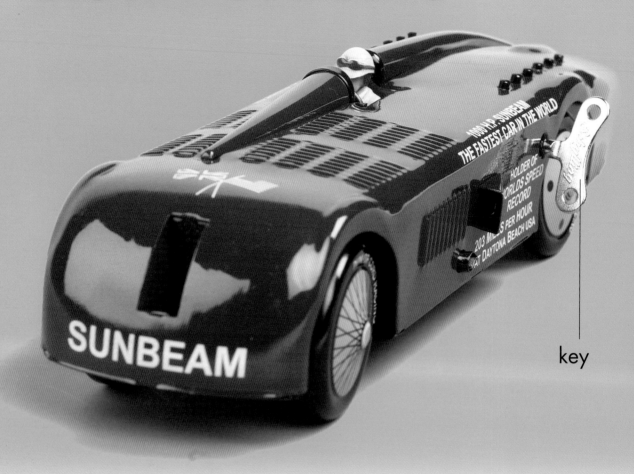

key

Everything that moves needs **energy**. This car has a **spring** inside it. When you turn the key, you tighten up the spring inside the car.

spring unwinds

When you let go
of the key on a
clockwork car,
the spring
inside unwinds.

When you wind up a **clockwork** car,
the spring wants to go back to the shape
it was before. When you let go of the
key, the spring unwinds and makes the
wheels of the car go round.

Battery cars

energy from the battery makes the lights work

energy from the battery makes the wheels turn

Some toy cars get their **energy** from **electricity**. A **battery** inside the car makes the electricity. This makes the wheels go round. Batteries can also be used to make sounds or make lights come on.

Some cars move without you touching them. They are called **remote-control** cars. You use electricity to send a signal to the car. The signal tells the car how to move. Remote-control cars usually need batteries to make them work.

Cars on tracks

These cars do not have **batteries** inside them. They get **electricity** from the **track**. The electricity makes the cars move.

There are **slots** in the middle of each track.
The cars sit in these slots to get electricity.
If a car comes off the track, it will have
no electricity and will stop moving.

Bits and pieces

All these parts
were used to
make just one
toy car. Can
you work
out where
all the pieces
should go?

Find out more about toy cars at
www.heinemannexplore.co.uk

29

Glossary

axle rod that holds a wheel but still lets the wheel turn round

battery something that stores electricity

clockwork using a spring to store energy

electricity kind of energy used for lighting, heating, and making machines work

energy something that is used to make things move

orce push or pull that makes something move or stops it moving

gravity force that pulls everything down towards the ground

grip hold without slipping

lever simple machine that makes it easier to move something

remote control way of working a machine from a distance

slot small opening that something else can fit into

spring something that can be pressed or pulled, but that always returns to the shape it was before

steering wheel wheel that you turn with your hands to make the wheels of a car turn

track rail used by some toy cars to get power for moving

Find out more

More books to read

Tremendous Toy Trucks, Les Neufeld (The Taunton Press, 2001)

Usbourne Beginners Series: Trucks (Usbourne Publishing Ltd, 2003)

Very Useful Machines: Levers, Chris Oxlade (Heinemann Library, 2004)

Very Useful Machines: Wheels, Chris Oxlade (Heinemann Library, 2004)

What Was It Like in the Past: Toys, Kamini Khanduri (Heinemann Library, 2002)

Websites to visit

http://www.matchbox.com
Visit the 'Gamezone' of this toy cars website to play some games.

http://www.howstuffworks.com
This website has lots of information about how cars and wheels work.

Disclaimer

All the Internet addresses (URLs) given in this book were valid at the time of going to press. However, due to the dynamic nature of the Internet, some addresses may have changed, or sites may have changed or ceased to exist since publication. While the author and Publishers regret any inconvenience this may cause readers, no responsibility for any such changes can be accepted by either the author or the Publishers.

Index